# Fieldwork Investigations 2
## The Natural Environment
## Sue Warn

# Contents

**Introduction** ..................................... 3

**Geological Investigations**
Rates of Weathering ................................. 4
Limestone Pavements ............................... 5
Shakeholes .......................................... 6
Effects of Faulting .................................. 7
Cross-profiles of a Dry Valley ...................... 8
Assessing the Value of a Landscape ............... 8

**Weather Investigations**
Running a Weather Station ........................ 10
Recording Weather Changes ...................... 13
Microclimate Investigations in
    Your Garden .................................. 15
Microclimate Investigations in
    a School or College .......................... 16
Microclimate Investigations in
    Your Local Area ............................... 17

**Investigating Soils**
Soil Sampling Methods ............................ 19
Testing Soil Characteristics ...................... 20
Soil-profile Studies ............................... 23
Analysing the Results of a Soil Transect ........ 24

**Investigating the Vegetation**
Before You Begin .................................. 26
How to Sample Vegetation ........................ 26
What to Record at Each Site ..................... 27
Presenting the Results ........................... 28
Woodland Survey .................................. 30
Hedgerow Survey .................................. 32

ARNOLD - WHEATON

# FIELDWORK INVESTIGATIONS 2

Arnold-Wheaton
*A Division of E.J. Arnold & Son Limited*
Parkside Lane, Leeds LS11 5TD

A subsidiary of Pergamon Press Ltd
Headington Hill Hall, Oxford OX3 0BW

Pergamon Press Inc.
Maxwell House, Fairview Park, Elmsford, New York 10523

Pergamon Press Canada Ltd
Suite 104, 150 Consumers Road, Willowdale, Ontario M2J 1P9

Pergamon Press (Australia) Pty Ltd
P.O. Box 544, Potts Point, N.S.W. 2011

Pergamon Press GmbH
Hammerweg 6, D-6242 Kronberg, Federal Republic of Germany

Copyright © 1985 Sue Warn

All rights reserved.
No part of this publication may be reproduced, stored in a
retrieval system, or transmitted, in any form or by any
means, electronic, electrostatic, magnetic tape, mechanical,
photocopying, recording or otherwise, without permission
in writing from the publishers.

First published 1985

Printed in Great Britain by A. Wheaton & Co. Ltd, Hennock Road, Exeter

ISBN 0 560-66501-6

Acknowledgements
The author would like to thank the warden, Mr E. Jones, and staff of Hothersall Lodge, the Lancashire County Field Study Centre, for their help and advice; also students at Nelson and Colne College and Habergham High School, Burnley, and Mr D. Richardson, Geography Tutor at Hothersall Lodge, for their help with photographs and fieldwork.

Layout and illustration by Denby Designs

# INTRODUCTION

Fig. 1. The natural environment

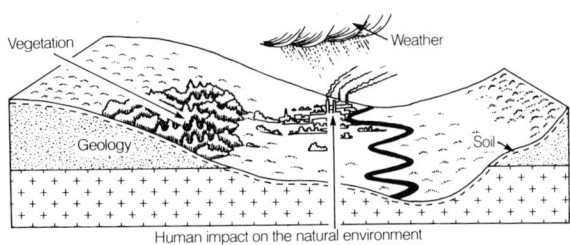

## What Can You Investigate?

Fig. 1 shows the main parts of the natural environmental system. It is possible to choose a project which investigates one part of the system or to study the interaction of several parts of the system within a limited area: for example, you could relate changes in vegetation to rock type and soil across a valley. For many natural environment investigations you will require equipment in order to obtain sufficiently accurate results, therefore your project choice may be limited by the availability of particular items. Increasingly, equipment for studying soils, vegetation and the weather is becoming available in versions suitable for use in schools. Also, it is possible to develop home-made substitutes in some cases: for example quadrats for vegetation sampling.

## Choosing a Project

Fig. 2 shows you the stages to follow when carrying out your investigations. Probably the most important is making thorough *preparations*: checking on equipment, deciding on a location, and working out how many measurements to make.

## General Check-list

- Maps.
- Equipment.
- Booking-forms.
- Suitable clothing for outdoor work.
- Textbooks from library for extra information.
- Transport arrangements.
- Helpers with fieldwork.
- Permission from land-owners.

## Safety

Although it is unlikely that you will be working in a remote area, there are nevertheless important general safety precautions you have to take when working in the country.

- Never work alone.
- Always tell an adult exactly where you will be working.
- Always take warm and waterproof clothing with you, in case of a change in weather, and wear strong footwear.

Fig. 2. Choosing a project – the route of enquiry

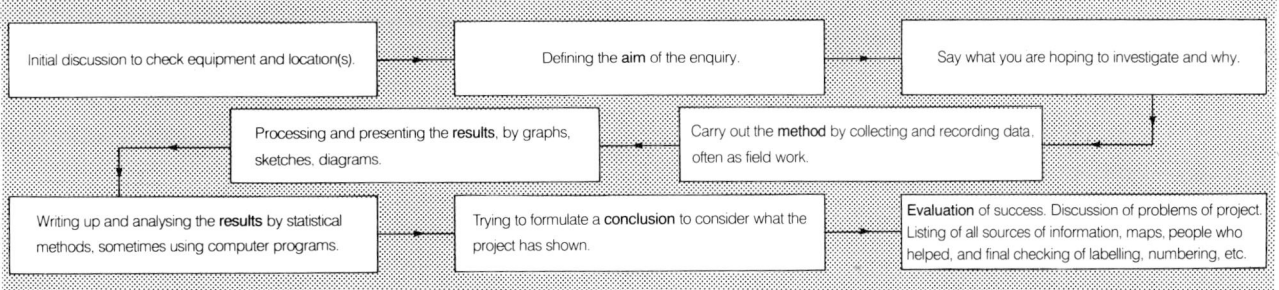

# GEOLOGICAL INVESTIGATIONS

Although you do not have to be studying geology to carry out a successful geological project, you will need a simple geology guide to help you recognize the rock types in your study area. One with colour pictures of common pebbles is a great help. Always try to look at a fresh 'wetted' face of rock, by cracking open a pebble and putting it under a tap, as weathering frequently changes a rock's colour. You will also need access to a geology map of your area. 'Solid' maps show the geology as it would appear if there were no deposits of river silt or glacial boulder clay dumped on top, whereas 'drift' maps show all these deposits, which in lowland areas usually cover the underlying rocks.

The nature of a rock, known as its **lithology**, will affect its ability to withstand weathering and erosion. You should consider the chemical make-up of the rock – for example, is it soluble like limestone? The permeability determines whether water can move through the rock, and the degree of jointing can influence the rate of weathering.

## Safety

- When hammering always use protective glasses and wear a hard helmet.
- Never stand underneath a rock face.
- Never work in a quarry without permission.
- Always work with a friend because old quarries are dangerous places.

## Measuring Rates of Weathering

It is almost impossible to measure rates of either physical or chemical weathering accurately with cheap, home-made equipment. One useful technique is to visit a local graveyard, study the date on each gravestone, record its rock type, and see which class you can put it into from Table 1. This gives you an idea of the time it takes for various rock types to weather.

### Project Ideas

1. Comparative quarry surveys – studies of the impact, nature and operation of two or more contrasting quarries (see Book 3).
2. Building-stone surveys – especially of the use and distribution of a localized rock type.
3. Surveys at the coast to assess the impact of rock type on the coastal features (see Book 1).
4. Surveys to assess the effect of rock type on scenery. These usually involve a transect across varied countryside to see how the rock type has affected soils, vegetation, drainage and land use.

Table 1. Scale of weathering on gravestones

| Class | Description |
|---|---|
| 1 | Looks almost brand new – unweathered |
| 2 | Slightly weathered – some letters just beginning to get rounded corners |
| 3 | Moderately weathered – rough surface but letters can be read |
| 4 | Badly weathered – letters difficult to read |
| 5 | Very badly weathered – letters impossible to read |
| 6 | Extremely weathered – no letters left, gravestone breaking up |

# GEOLOGICAL INVESTIGATIONS

# LIMESTONE AREAS

Certain rock types such as chalk, hard limestone or clay have very characteristic scenery. In the case of limestone, the rock is pervious, chemically weathered along joints and bedding-planes, and resistant to erosion, usually forming uplands. The unusual surface and subsurface features such as limestone pavements and caves make a very interesting study. Limestone scenery is known as **KARST**.

## Project Ideas

1. Make a detailed survey of the nature and characteristics of limestone pavements.
2. Study the distribution and nature of shakeholes.
3. Investigate the effects of faulting upon the surface features.
4. Survey cross-profiles of dry valleys and relate them to erosional processes.
5. Survey the drainage systems of limestone areas.

## Limestone Pavements

Limestone pavements are exposures of limestone bedrock divided into blocks (clints) by the intersection of chemically widened joints (grykes). One idea is to study two areas of limestone pavement to see how and why the nature of the pavement varies.

## Equipment Check-list

- Collapsible quadrat 1 m × 1 m.
- Clinometer for measuring dip of rocks.
- Spiked broom-handle, marked every 10 cm, for measuring gryke depth.
- Compass to find orientation of major joints.
- Base map to record sites surveyed.
- Measuring-tape.

Photo 1. Surveying a limestone pavement

*Gradual growth of vegetation in the grykes.*
*Wooden quadrat for sampling*
*Clint*
*Gryke*

You will not be able to study every clint and gryke, so you will have to sample a small number. This can be done in two ways. Photo 1 shows a student using a quadrat. Twenty quadrats were sampled in a ¼ km × ¼ km area. A second way is to survey a transect across the pavement to show variations in clint width and gryke depth. Gryke depth is measured by using a spiked broom-handle. The results can be best shown by drawing an accurate cross-section of the limestone pavement. Table 2 lists the measurements to obtain at each recording site in order to do a thorough survey.

Table 2. Features of limestone pavements

| Feature | Measurements to make | How to display results | Questions to answer |
|---|---|---|---|
| Vegetation cover | % of quadrat covered by vegetation | Pie charts | To what extent is the vegetation cover influenced by the geology? |
| Pavement size | Length of long axis of each clint in quadrat | Histogram | Do clints vary in size? |
| Runnels | % of clint cut into by runnels and hollows | Scattergram | Are runnels more common in steeply sloping clints? |
| Grykes | Gryke depth<br>% of quadrat occupied by grykes<br>Width of grykes | Histograms | Are deeper grykes associated with larger pavements?<br>Is there a distinct pattern of major jointing? |

# GEOLOGICAL INVESTIGATIONS

## Shakeholes

Shakeholes are cone-shaped depressions about 3 m deep and 9 m across. They look like bomb craters and occur where limestone is covered with glacial boulder clay; water moving downhill dissolves the rock. Provided you keep away from the very dangerous, large shakeholes, they are an interesting small-scale feature about which you can find a lot of information. Try to explain variations in their size, shape and orientation by surveying about fifteen examples in one area.

### Project Ideas

1. Are shakeholes the same size and shape? Are long narrow ones formed along joints, whereas round ones occur at the junction of two joints?
2. To what extent are larger shakeholes found on gentle slopes, where there is less surface run-off and more water pouring down the hole?
3. Are shakeholes orientated in any one direction (e.g. NW – SE)? Is orientation related to slope or jointing pattern?
4. Do larger shakeholes drain larger catchment areas?

### Equipment Check-list

- Compass.
- Clinometer.
- Measuring-tape.
- Tent-pegs.
- Clothes-line marked off every 50 cm.
- Polythene bags for soil samples.
- Booking-sheets.

### Measurements to Make

1. Mark the position of each shakehole on your map by reference to features such as walls and roads.
2. Decide which is the long axis and measure it as shown in Fig. 3. Then measure the short axis, which is the maximum diameter at right angles to the long axis. Calculate the **elongation ratio**:

    $$\text{elongation ratio} = \frac{\text{long axis}}{\text{short axis}}$$

    An answer of 1 indicates a round shakehole.

Fig. 3. How to survey a shakehole

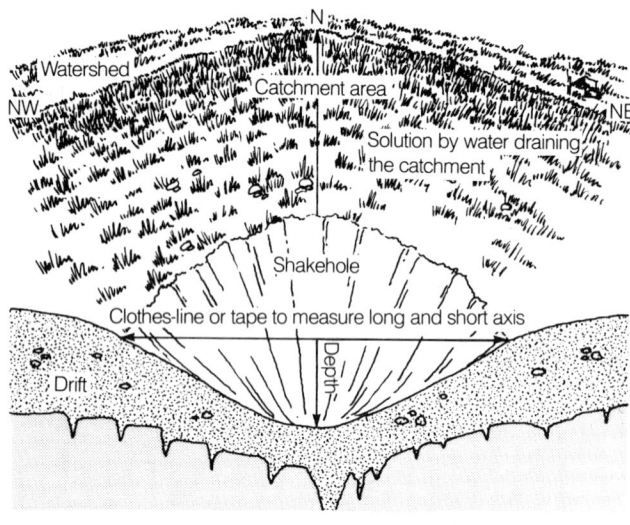

3. Measure the depth by suspending a tape as shown in Fig. 3.
4. Use the compass to record the orientation (in degrees) of the long axis.
5. Use the clinometer to record the angle of the steepest slope into the shakehole.
6. Investigate the bottom of the shakehole and, if possible, measure soil depth. Place a soil sample in a polythene bag and test the pH and moisture content back at school.
7. Calculate the size of the shakehole. Use the long and short axis measurements to find the radius.

    $$\text{radius} = \frac{\text{long axis} + \text{short axis}}{2}$$

    $$\text{shakehole size} = \text{radius}^2 \times \pi$$

8. The catchment area is the area from where water drains into the shakehole. Place marker pegs around the watershed to help you make a scale plan. This technique is explained in an article by Dr. K. Paterson in **Geography**, April 1980.

Fig. 4 shows a booking-form for recording the main features of each shakehole.

# GEOLOGICAL INVESTIGATIONS

Fig. 4. Booking sheet for features of a shakehole

| Hole number | Length of long axis (m) | Orientation of long axis | Depth (m) | Length of short axis (m) | Slope angle (deg) | Mean diameter (m) | Elongation ratio | Catchment area (m$^2$) |
|---|---|---|---|---|---|---|---|---|
| 1 | 6.60 m | 120° | 1.70 m | 6.20 m | 4° | 6.40 | 1.06 | 36 m$^2$ |
| 2 | 14.00 m | 135° | 1.75 m | 10.30 m | 4° | 12.15 | 1.36 | 52 m$^2$ |
| 3 | 7.90 m | 110° | 2.00 m | 5.90 m | 9° | 6.9 | 1.34 | 120 m$^2$ |
| 4 | 11.90 m | 135° | 3.00 m | 8.40 m | 5° | 10.15 | 1.42 | 32 m$^2$ |
| 5 | 7.40 m | 105° | 1.25 m | 5.90 m | 7° | 6.65 | 1.25 | 58 m$^2$ |
| 6 | 9.00 m | 32° | 1.60 m | 5.00 m | 3° | 7.00 | 1.8 | 87 m$^2$ |
| 7 | 8.50 m | 4° | 1.50 m | 6.60 m | 2° | 7.55 | 1.29 | 142 m$^2$ |
| 8 | 8.70 m | 106° | 1.25 m | 5.60 m | 2° | 7.15 | 1.55 | 119 m$^2$ |
| 9 | 7.20 m | 130° | 1.75 m | 6.00 m | 11° | 6.60 | 1.2 | 61 m$^2$ |

## Presentation of Results
1. Bar graphs to show variations in the long and short axis.
2. Scatter graphs to show elongation ratios.
3. Rose diagrams showing the orientation of the long axis.
4. Scatter graphs relating depth to catchment area.
5. A detailed sketch-map to show locations.

## Survey of the Effects of Faulting

Use a geology map to mark the line of the fault in detail on a 1:10 000 base map. Then conduct a series of surveys at about ten points on each side of the fault, as shown in Photo 2.

Photo 2. Surveying a fault line

# GEOLOGICAL INVESTIGATIONS

## *Suggested Measurements at Each Point*

1. Construct a cross-section from the map or a slope profile (see Book 1) to see the effect of the fault upon relief.
2. Find where a stream crosses the fault. Study the stream's discharge and its features above and below the fault to see if there are any differences (see Book 1).
3. Conduct soil surveys (see page 20) to compare soil texture, depth, pH, moisture and humus content on either side of the fault. Take samples about 100 m away from the fault line.
4. Undertake vegetation surveys (see page 27) to see whether the vegetation varies as a result of the faulting.
5. Survey land use – compare land use, stocking rates, and land-use capability on either side of the fault (see Book 3).

## Cross-profiles of a Dry Valley

For one dry valley, try to identify the major slopes and the processes operating on those slopes. Accurate results are more likely if you survey a number of cross-profiles (six, say).

## *Suggested Measurements*

1. Mark the site of each profile on a base map. Add to this the position of major features such as cliffs, caves, scree and limestone pavements.
2. Survey the slopes of the cross-section (see Book 1), noting changes in gradient, surface material, vegetation and height.

## Assessing the Value of a Landscape

It is possible to evaluate the quality of every landscape as a *whole*. There are a number of factors which need to be considered. For instance, in Photo 3 there is not great variety in the landscape but, apart from agriculture, it is relatively free from man-made features. You can make up an evaluation sheet similar to Fig. 5 and try to quantify (by using a points system) the quality of each area. The problem is that when you start to consider 'intrinsic appeal', not everybody has the same views as to the attractiveness of scenery. Try this out on Photo 3 with a friend, and see what scores you each give it. An overall picture can be obtained by averaging the scores of at least five people.

Photo 3. A Pennine landscape

# GEOLOGICAL INVESTIGATIONS

Fig. 5. Landscape evaluation sheet

| Location.................................... Kilometre square number .................................... |||
|---|---|---|
| Items to evaluate || Score |
| 1. What percentage of the area is open space?<br>Score 1 point for each 10% identified as open space. || |
| 2. What variety of features is there in the square?<br>Score 1 point for each of the following features identified:<br><br>cliffs, valley, marsh, waterfall, cave, moorland, hills, lake, river, flood plain, wood, beach, sea || |
| 3. What variety of flora and fauna is there in the square?<br>How many different species of plants and animals can you identify?<br>Use a good reference book. Score up to 10 points for the greatest variety. || |
| 4. What is the intrinsic appeal of the area?<br>How do you feel about it? Is it pretty, boring, exciting, ugly or awful?<br>Do you like the area?<br><br>Here are five pairs of opposites to choose between. For instance, if you thought the area was quite beautiful, you would score 2 points. An ugly area would score no points.<br><br>\| Appealing \| Points \| Unappealing \|<br>\|---\|---\|---\|<br>\| Beautiful \| 3 2 1 0 \| Ugly \|<br>\| Interesting \| 3 2 1 0 \| Boring \|<br>\| Spectacular \| 3 2 1 0 \| Dull \|<br>\| Varied \| 3 2 1 0 \| Monotonous \|<br>\| Inviting \| 3 2 1 0 \| Hostile \| || Total for<br>Items 1 – 4 .............. |
| 5. What effect have people had on the landscape?<br>Man-made features usually spoil an area. Look at each feature, e.g. pylons, houses, walls, factories, roads, hedges, and see how it scores on this scale:<br><br>\| Blends in with environment \| no points deducted \|<br>\|---\|---\|<br>\| Only a little impact on environment \| 1 point deducted \|<br>\| Strong impact on environment \| 2 points deducted \|<br>\| Pollutes the environment \| 3 points deducted \| || Deduct<br>points for<br>Item 5  ..............<br><br>Total score  .............. |

## Project Idea

Are the most beautiful areas under the greatest threat?

Choose an area of open countryside about 5 km × 5 km and use a map to divide it into 25 kilometre squares. For each square, carry out an assessment as shown in Fig. 5 and take a photograph – always from the same corner of each square. This can be used for testing intrinsic appeal. You will then be able to score a total for each square. Next carry out a survey of the density of people using the area for recreation on a busy summer day to see whether the areas of greatest quality are the most heavily used (see Book 3). You can also carry out litter, trampling and erosion surveys to investigate whether the most attractive areas are under the greatest threat.

# Weather Investigations

## Project Ideas

There are two major types of weather investigation:

1. Set up a **weather station** and carry out a full range of accurate recordings over a continuous period of time – a minimum of two weeks is recommended. The weather instruments must be correctly sited and must be read at the *same* time each day: for example, 9.00 a.m. or 9.00 p.m. For this reason, they need to be placed in a large back garden or very near your home, on a vandal-free site.
2. Record aspects of the weather, such as temperature, over a wider area: for example, across a valley. The big problem here is that you need more than one of each item of equipment – for example, twelve thermometers for twelve sites – or transport and a group of friends to help you cover the area efficiently. This type of investigation is really a study of climate variations on a small scale and is known as a **microclimate** investigation.

## Running a Weather Station
### Choosing a Site

A Stevenson screen provides a sheltered, shaded atmosphere for recording air temperatures accurately. It is possible to construct a home-made substitute from a well-ventilated light-coloured bread-bin.
Simple precautions are:

- Avoid overhanging trees, especially for the rain gauge, which should be sited in a grassy area.
- Site your weather station on open grassland and avoid concrete and tarmac.
- Ensure that the Stevenson screen, or box, is over 1 metre above the ground.

## Temperature

Always measure temperature in degrees centigrade. To record **ground temperature**, use a minimum thermometer placed horizontally and supported with pegs a few centimetres above the soil. You will notice a much greater variation in temperature at ground level – it will be hotter by day and cooler by night compared with the **air temperature** which you record inside the Stevenson screen by reading the maximum and minimum thermometer. The **daily temperature range** is the difference between the maximum and minimum air temperatures recorded each day.

## Wind Speed

Wind speed can be measured in a variety of ways. The simplest method requires no equipment and is based on the Beaufort Scale shown in Table 3. Look around, especially at trees, and relate what you see, hear and feel to the descriptions for each wind force.

Table 3. The Beaufort Scale of wind force

| Beaufort number | Descriptive title | Effect on land features |
|---|---|---|
| 0 | Calm | Smoke rises vertically |
| 1 | Light air | Direction shown by smoke but not wind vanes |
| 2 | Light breeze | Wind felt on face; leaves rustle; vane moves |
| 3 | Gentle breeze | Leaves and twigs in constant motion |
| 4 | Moderate breeze | Raises dust and paper; small branches moved |
| 5 | Fresh breeze | Small trees begin to sway |
| 6 | Strong breeze | Large branches in motion; whistling in telephone wires |
| 7 | Moderate gale | Whole trees in motion |
| 8 | Fresh gale | Breaks twigs off trees |
| 9 | Strong gale | Slight structural damage to roofs, etc. |
| 10 | Whole gale | Trees uprooted; considerable structural damage |
| 11 | Storm | Widespread damage |
| 12 | Hurricane | Widespread devastation |

# WEATHER INVESTIGATIONS

The cheapest piece of equipment which records wind speeds is a **ventimeter**, obtainable from a sailing-shop. Wind blows across a tube, causing a pointer to rise up the tube and indicate the wind speed.

The most sophisticated instrument for reading wind speed is an **anemometer**. This has revolving cups connected to a recording meter which counts the rotations in a given period of time. Photo 4 shows a hand-held version. It is possible to make your own anemometer using three yoghurt pots, one of which should be of a different colour. Count the number of times this coloured cup passes in a given period to get an idea of relative wind speeds.

Cloud type is recorded by looking at a picture chart, available in any basic weather guide.

## Visibility

In clear weather, prepare a sketch-map of the landmarks around your weather station like Fig. 6. Factories, churches and pylons all make clearly recognized landmarks. Use an Ordnance Survey map to work out the straight-line distance of each feature from your weather station.

Fog is said to occur when you cannot see for 1 km. Therefore, from Fig. 6, if the church is not visible, then it is foggy.

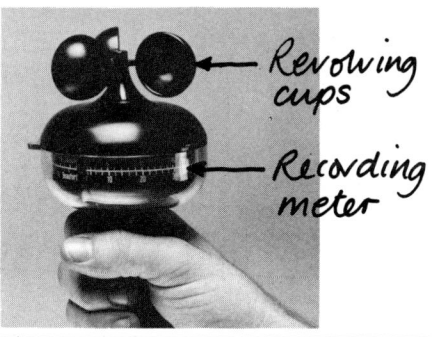

Photo 4. A hand-held anemometer

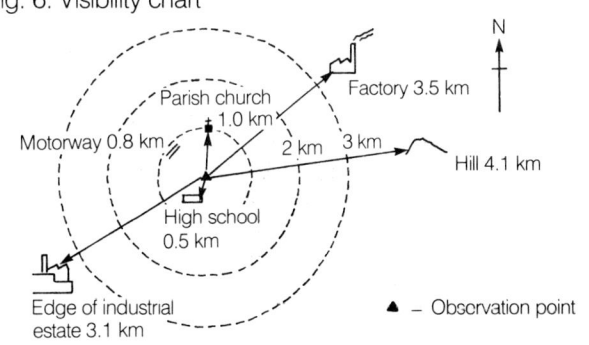

Fig. 6. Visibility chart

## Wind Direction

Wind direction is indicated by a wind vane. The pointer shows the direction from which the wind is blowing. Our most frequent wind in Great Britain is the southwesterly – it is the prevailing wind and blows from the south-west. The simplest way of measuring wind direction is to use a flag or streamer. Before you begin your series of measurements, mark the points of the compass in chalk on the ground.

## Cloud Cover and Type

The amount of cloud is recorded by estimating what fraction of the sky is covered by cloud. This is expressed in eighths of cover, and the units are known as oktas. For example, when three-quarters of the sky is covered, it is said to have six oktas of cloud.

## Sunshine

The amount and intensity of sunshine have a very important effect on plant growth. The standard instrument for measuring hours of sun is a Campbell-Stokes recorder. When the sun shines, the rays are focused by a glass ball so as to make a burn mark on a strip of paper. The longer the length of the burn mark, the more sunshine there has been. As this instrument is rarely available in school, an alternative is to measure light intensity, using a photographer's light meter. Set the aperture (f) to f8, and record the speed reading. The faster the speed, the greater the light intensity. Very interesting projects can be done which involve looking at the variations in light intensity in built-up areas, or in a wood (see Fig. 34).

# WEATHER INVESTIGATIONS

## Precipitation

In Britain, the most common form of precipitation is rain, which can be measured using either a home-made rain gauge constructed from a plastic lemonade bottle, or a simple plastic gauge sold by school-equipment firms such as E.J. Arnold. Record the rainfall in millimetres at the same time each day.

Snow depth can be measured with a ruler, with 10 mm of snow representing a 1 mm fall of rain.

## Humidity

Humidity is the amount of water vapour in the atmosphere, and can be measured by three main instruments, all of which are available in a cheap version:

1. A **wet and dry thermometer** consists of two thermometers, one of which has its bulb wrapped in a muslin wick dipped in water. If the air is not saturated (i.e. completely full of water vapour), water will evaporate from the muslin, thus cooling the thermometer and lowering the temperature. The relative humidity can be found by using Table 4. For example, if the dry bulb thermometer registers 10°C and the wet bulb thermometer registers 8.75°C, the difference is 1.25°C, giving a relative humidity of 86%.

2. A whirling **psychrometer** as shown in Photo 5. This consists of a wet and dry bulb thermometer mounted in a frame. If you swing this round and round like a football supporter's rattle for 1 min, evaporation from the wet bulb lowers the temperature. Find the relative humidity by using Table 4.

3. A **hygrometer** has a dial which records the relative humidity directly.

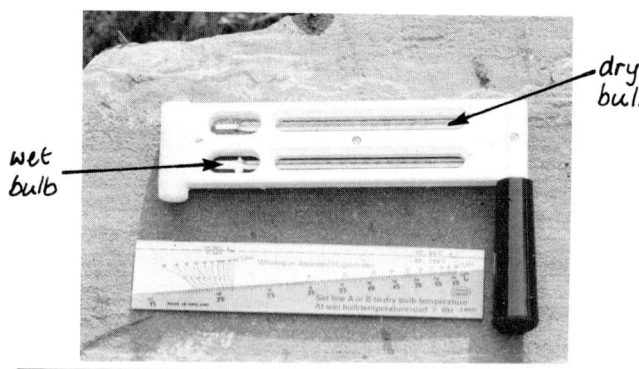

Photo 5. A whirling psychrometer

Table 4. How to work out relative humidity

Difference in temperature between dry and wet bulb (°C)

| Dry bulb temp. | 0.25 | 0.5 | 0.75 | 1.0 | 1.25 | 1.50 | 1.75 | 2.0 | 2.25 | 2.50 | 2.75 | 3.0 | 3.25 | 3.5 | 3.75 | 4.0 |
|---|---|---|---|---|---|---|---|---|---|---|---|---|---|---|---|---|
| 4 | 96 | 92 | 89 | 85 | 82 | 78 | 74 | 70 | 67 | 63 | 60 | 56 | 53 | 49 | 46 | 42 |
| 6 | 97 | 93 | 90 | 86 | 83 | 79 | 76 | 73 | 70 | 66 | 63 | 60 | 57 | 53 | 50 | 47 |
| 8 | 97 | 94 | 91 | 89 | 85 | 81 | 78 | 75 | 72 | 69 | 66 | 63 | 60 | 57 | 54 | 51 |
| 10 | 97 | 94 | 91 | 88 | 86 | 82 | 79 | 76 | 74 | 71 | 68 | 65 | 63 | 60 | 58 | 54 |
| 12 | 98 | 94 | 91 | 89 | 87 | 83 | 80 | 78 | 75 | 73 | 70 | 68 | 65 | 62 | 59 | 57 |
| 14 | 98 | 95 | 92 | 90 | 87 | 84 | 81 | 79 | 77 | 74 | 72 | 70 | 67 | 65 | 62 | 60 |
| 16 | 98 | 95 | 92 | 90 | 88 | 85 | 83 | 81 | 78 | 76 | 73 | 71 | 69 | 67 | 65 | 63 |
| 18 | 98 | 95 | 93 | 91 | 89 | 86 | 83 | 82 | 79 | 77 | 75 | 73 | 71 | 69 | 67 | 65 |
| 20 | 98 | 96 | 93 | 91 | 89 | 87 | 85 | 83 | 80 | 78 | 76 | 74 | 72 | 70 | 67 | 66 |
| 22 | 98 | 96 | 94 | 92 | 90 | 88 | 85 | 83 | 81 | 80 | 78 | 76 | 74 | 72 | 70 | 68 |
| 24 | 98 | 96 | 94 | 92 | 90 | 88 | 86 | 84 | 82 | 80 | 78 | 77 | 75 | 73 | 71 | 69 |

# WEATHER INVESTIGATIONS

## *Air Pressure*

Air pressure is recorded by a barometer. The cheaper types are aneroid barometers. Always read the pressure in millibars. High pressure is linked with fair weather. If the pressure starts to fall when you 'tap' the barometer this indicates the onset of more unsettled conditions. A reading of around 960 mb is a very low pressure and there may be very stormy weather.

## Recording Weather Changes

Fig. 7 is an example of a weather booking-sheet. Draw up your own to include all the measurements you will make. Once you have completed your measurements the results can be displayed in a variety of ways. Fig. 8 and Fig. 9 portray the results of recordings during two weeks in July. Fig. 8 shows temperature and rainfall, while Fig. 9 is a wind rose diagram which shows the force and direction of the wind for that two-week period.

Fig. 7. Booking sheet for daily weather observations

| Date | Time | Temperature Max. (°C) | Min. (°C) | Wet bulb (°C) | Dry bulb (°C) | Cloud cover (oktas) | Pressure (mb) | Wind strength (Beaufort scale) | Wind direction | Rainfall (mm) | Sunshine (h) | Comments |
|---|---|---|---|---|---|---|---|---|---|---|---|---|
| 26 July | 9.00 am | 22 | 13 | 10 | 16 | 2 | 1016 | 3 | SE | Nil | 8.4 | Fine, sunny day. |
| 27 July | 9.00 a.m | 26 | 14 | 18 | 19 | 6 | 1004 | 6 | SW | 69 | 7.2 | Storm overnight, still raining. |

Fig. 8. Temperature and rainfall for two weeks in July

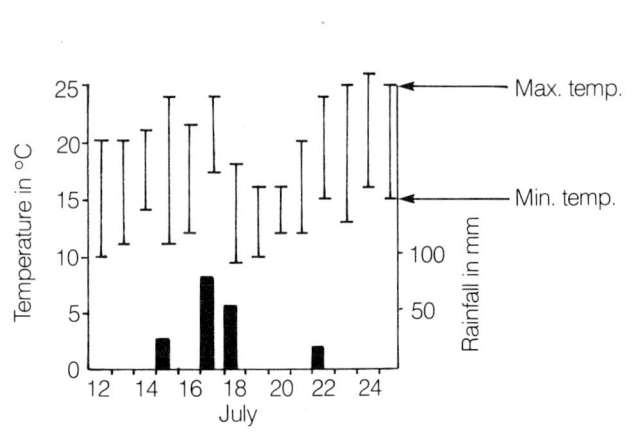

Fig. 9. Windspeed and direction for two weeks in July

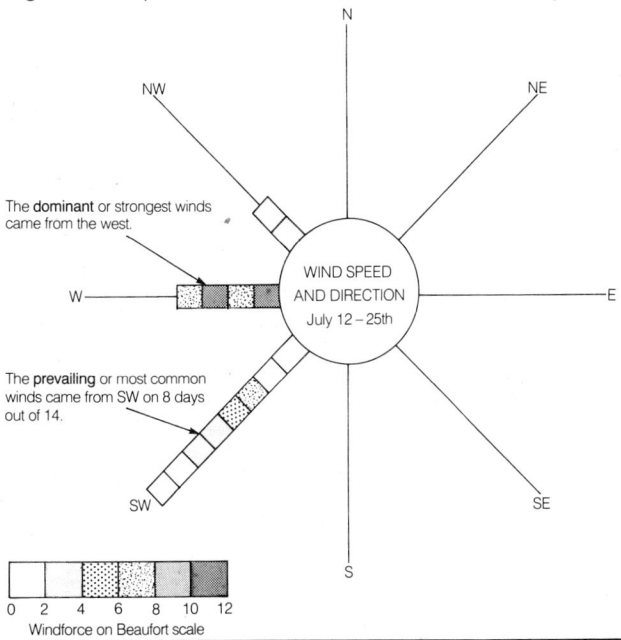

# WEATHER INVESTIGATIONS

## Project Ideas

1. Relate your two-week investigation to the wider pattern of weather in Great Britain by studying the television and newspaper forecasts. Reference to weather textbooks will show you how to recognize the two main weather systems operating in Great Britain. High-pressure systems, or anticyclones, usually produce calm, settled weather patterns with little change over a week. Depressions, or low-pressure systems, produce very rapidly changing weather patterns with differences in temperature, rainfall, pressure and wind speed and direction. You can use newspaper weather maps and information from textbooks to analyse your results, and also to investigate the accuracy of the weather forecasts.

3. It may be possible, by using a rota of friends and family, to make a detailed study of the effects of a depression on your local weather by taking readings every 2 h over a 48 h period. Fig. 10 shows the results of a series of such measurements recording the approach and passage of a depression. You obviously need to pick your recording days very carefully by looking at the television charts and forecasts and selecting a period when a large depression is approaching. September, October or November should be good months to choose. You should also collect the relevant newspaper cuttings of weather maps. You could then study a 48 h period during an anticyclone and compare the two sets of results.

Fig. 10. Weather records during the passage of a depression

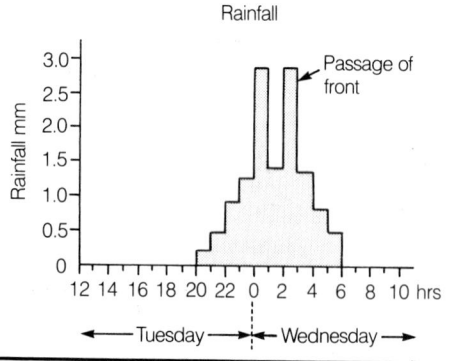
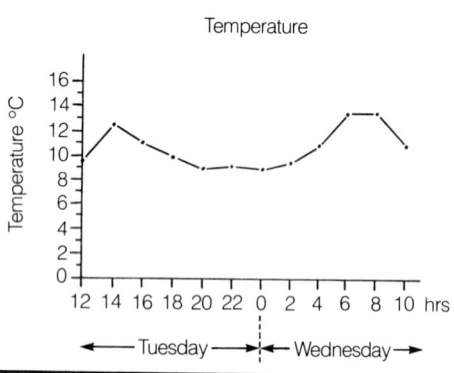

2. Compare your readings with those from one or two contrasting weather stations: for example, one at the coast and one in a city centre or a much hillier district. You could test one of the following ideas:

Is it milder and wetter at the coast?
Is there a big difference between highland and lowland weather?
How different is the weather in the city centre compared with the surrounding countryside?
Is there any evidence that the western sides of our major mountain ranges are wetter than the east?

For all these projects you will need to consult textbooks in order to explain the changes you have recorded.

Details of official recordings are usually available by post from your nearest Weather Centre. They are generally published about a month after the weather was recorded. However, it is always best to check which stations do provide information and what aspects of the weather are recorded *before* starting this project.

# WEATHER INVESTIGATIONS

# Microclimate Investigations

Microclimate studies involve measuring the changes in local weather conditions over a period of time. This section gives suggestions for working in your garden, school or local area.

## In Your Garden

### Project Idea

What variations in sunshine, temperature, wind strength, humidity and rainfall/snowfall can be noticed during the day or over a week in your garden and why?

There is no easier place to carry out these investigations than in a large varied back garden like the one in Fig. 11. You need to decide on the location of the sampling stations. Aim to have about ten different stations and carry out regular recordings at set times, maybe over a whole day for sunshine or several days for wind speed. In Fig. 11 the stations have been located to look at how factors such as the pond, trees, hedges, garden walls and buildings affect the microclimate.

Fig. 11. Microclimate surveys in a large garden

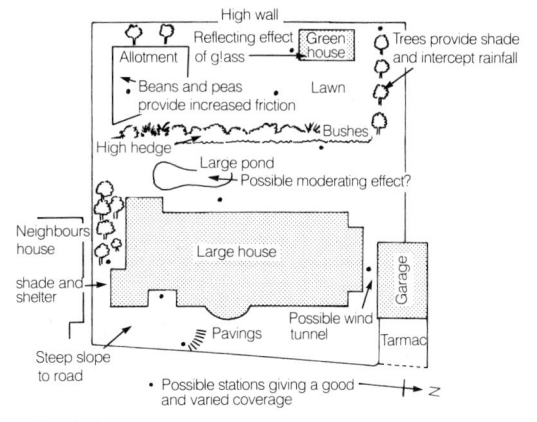

### Equipment Check-list

You need the following robust equipment which can be easily carried and quickly read:
- Thermometer.
- Light meter.
- Ventimeter.
- Hygrometer.
- One home-made rain gauge for each sampling station.

The results can be displayed on a map of the garden. For example, Fig. 12 shows the variations in total rainfall during the period of the study.

Fig. 12(a). Total rainfall for August

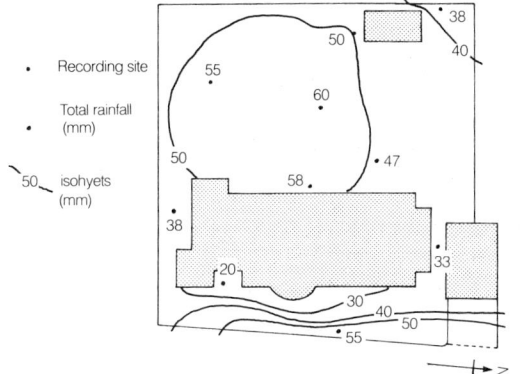

Fig. 12(b). Percentage variation from the maximum total rainfall for August

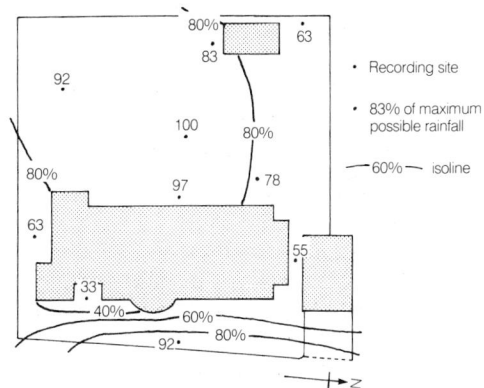

15

# WEATHER INVESTIGATIONS

If you have sited your instruments in good locations the results will show great differences. For instance, a north-east-facing corner may have no sunshine but an unshaded site may have 10 h each day.

An advanced, but very useful, method of showing variations in the microclimate is to use percentages. For example, 100 mm of rain may have been recorded at the centre of the lawn but only 40 mm at a sheltered site under a tree. The tree site is then said to have only 40% of the maximum rainfall. The percentages of the maximum rainfall received at each recording site in the garden can be shown on a map (see Fig. 12b).

## In a School or College

A school is an ideal site for investigations as you can get permission from your teachers to set up recording stations and most large schools also provide a great variety of microclimate environments. The high, complex buildings cause variations in sunshine, wind and rain, and the central-heating system has a major impact on temperature and humidity. Carry out a temperature survey every afternoon for a week in winter. The pattern in summer, when the central heating is off, should provide a major contrast, although the heat of 1000 bodies, and the effects of tarmac and concrete will still cause variations within the school site. Alternatively, you could contrast measurements for the morning, midday and late afternoon and try to account for any differences. Plot the results on a plan of the school in a similar way to that for the results recorded around a house.

Relate your results to surveys of the distribution of students at break and lunchtime in order to answer some of the following questions:
Do students gather in the most sheltered areas?
Do they sunbathe in the sunniest places?
Is there a relationship between student density and school-building temperature?

Fig. 13. Temperature variations around a school

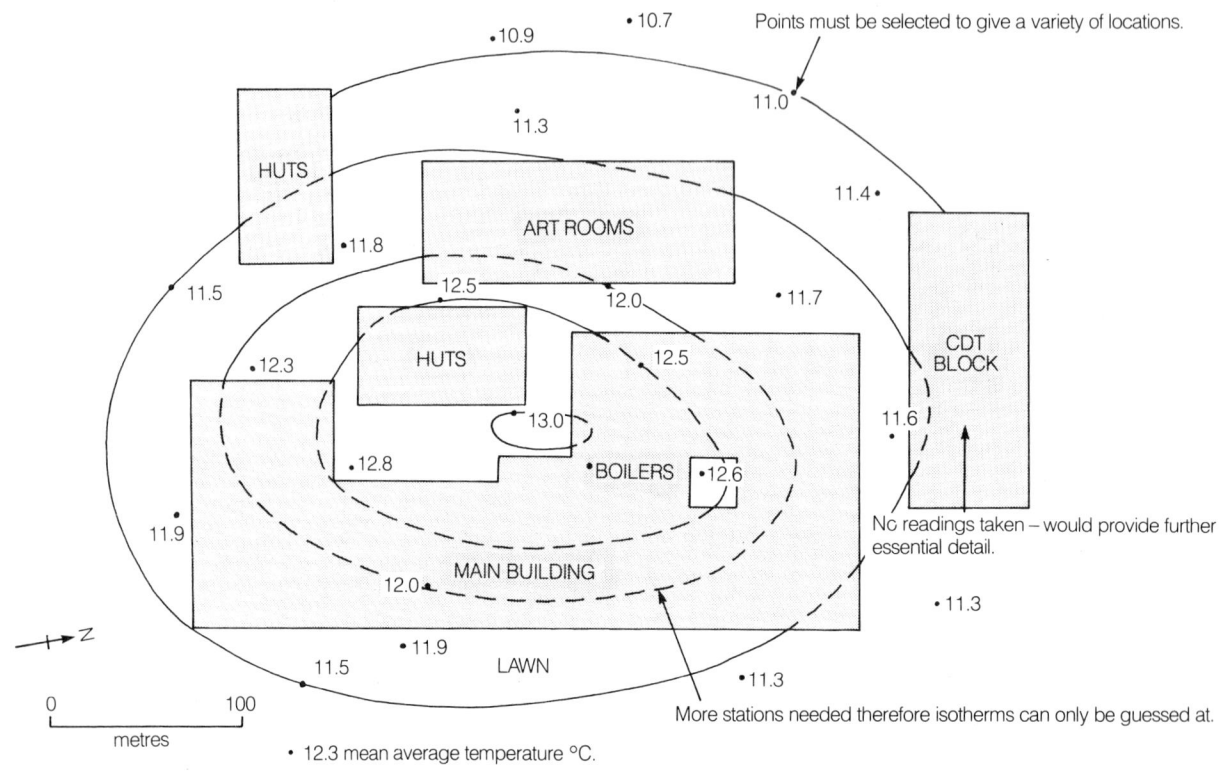

• 12.3 mean average temperature °C.

# WEATHER INVESTIGATIONS

## In Your Local Area

Fig. 14 shows how transects can be used in a small area in order to look at variations in local temperature, humidity, wind speed and light intensity. The main problem is that although these weather elements can be surveyed 'on the move' and do not require permanent weather stations, you may have to walk or cycle along the transect several times a day. Some weather elements, like fog, need to be surveyed over a wider area and for longer periods of time, and are therefore best suited to survey by a whole class.

The three transects in Fig. 14 show how the recording stations are carefully chosen to measure the impact of one major environmental feature on the local climate.

## Transect A: Across a Valley

### Project Ideas

1. How do temperatures vary during the day across the valley?

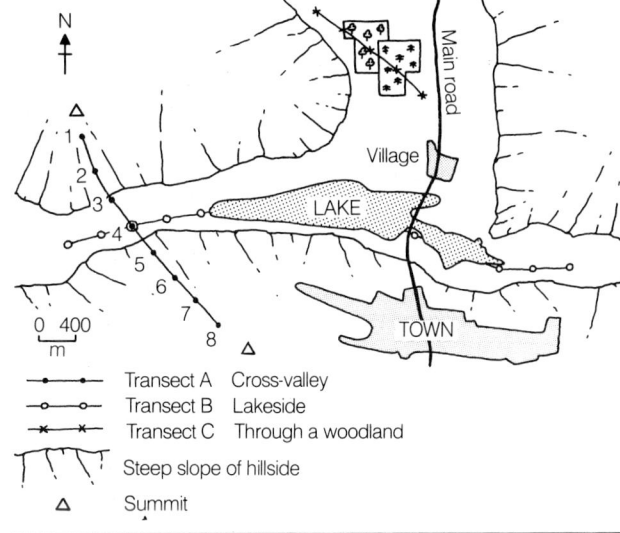

Fig. 14. Possible transects for microclimate study

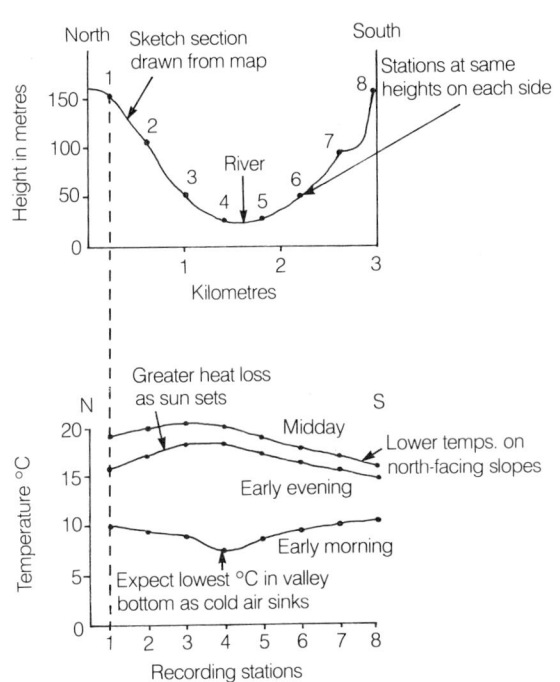

Fig. 15. Variations in temperature across a valley

2. Does aspect (the way the slope faces) affect the microclimate of the valley?
3. What effects does altitude have on the microclimate of the area? (In this case a detailed transect up one side of the valley is enough.)
4. How does the microclimate of the valley vary during the day and why? You will notice differences in wind direction as well here.

Choose a north-south transect if possible as this will give maximum contrast in temperature and light intensity. Avoid features such as a lake, which will have a major influence of its own. Select about ten stations at similar heights on each side of the valley as shown in Fig. 15. At each, record ground temperature, light intensity, wind speed, wind strength and humidity at the same times for several days, ideally in the early morning, around midday and in the early evening. The graph in Fig. 15 of the results of a temperature survey across the valley shows significant differences in all three sets of recordings. There would also be differences in the patterns of air pressure, light intensity, wind speed and wind direction, all of which could influence soil development, vegetation growth and the farmer's land-use decisions.

# WEATHER INVESTIGATIONS

## Transect B: Impact of a Lake on the Local Climate

### Project Ideas

1. What impact does the lake or reservoir have on the temperature range, humidity and rainfall?
2. Does the lake affect the pattern of frost and fog?

You need to take recordings both by the lake and at increasing distances away from it along the valley floor in order to see how the lake's influence decreases. Try to keep the stations at similar heights, and also on open ground. Obtain permission to site rain gauges on the land and then take readings of rainfall, temperature and humidity each morning and evening for several days. If possible, install maximum and minimum thermometers at these sites. In theory the lake should affect the microclimate patterns by having a warming influence in winter and a cooling influence in summer, and by adding considerably to the supply of water vapour in the atmosphere.

Also record the wind direction as this may cause contrasts in rainfall on either side of the lake, with the higher totals probably occurring downwind from the lake.

Early autumn or spring surveys are particularly interesting as you can use ground-temperature recordings (see page 10) to measure the occurrence and severity of frosts. These projects require mini weather stations to be set up, and are ideal for students with good contacts with local farmers.

## Transect C: Through a Wood

### Project Ideas

1. How is the microclimate of the wood different from that of the surrounding area? Do the trees reduce the daily temperature range? Do they increase friction and cut wind speeds? Does transpiration from the leaves increase the relative humidity? Does the shade of the trees cut down the amount of sunshine? What impact does the tree canopy have on precipitation?
2. Do different types of woodland have different climatic effects?
3. What differences are there between the woodland climates on a winter and a summer day?

Begin your transect in open country, passing through the woodland area and out the other side, so that you can compare the climate of the woodland with that of the surrounding open country. Readings should be taken in the morning, at noon and in the early evening over a number of days. Try to record the ground temperature, the air temperature at least 1½ m above the ground, the humidity, the wind strength, the light intensity and, if you can get permission to set them up, results from rain gauges and maximum and minimum thermometers.

At each site you will also need to record the nature and density of the trees using quadrats (see page 27). You could make your measurements on four single days at different seasons, or during a period when the trees are just coming into leaf.

Fig. 16. Variations in weather near a lake

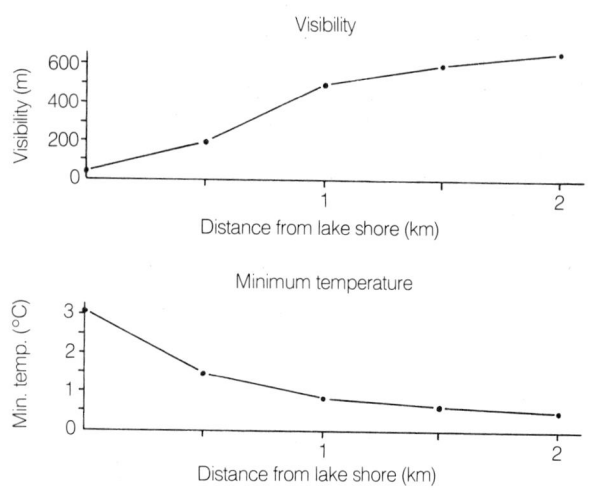

# Investigating Soils

Soil is made up of four main substances:

1. Broken-down rock.
2. Decayed vegetation.
3. Air.
4. Water.

In your local area you will find that the soil varies considerably even within small distances. This is because the factors which influence soil development may also have changed. The relief of the land affects drainage, the geology affects the mineral content, humans can alter the soil by ploughing and liming, while the vegetation affects the humus content.

## Project Ideas

By using about eight survey sites evenly spaced from the top to the bottom of a slope or across a river valley, you could investigate any of the following questions:

1. Are the soils wetter at the base of the slope?
2. How does soil moisture content relate to texture?
3. Are the soils deeper on the gentle slopes at the bottom of the valley?
4. Do changes in geology lead to changes in soil characteristics?
5. Are the most acid soils on the steepest slopes?
6. How does humus content vary down the slope?

Make sure you ask permission from the land-owner before you begin.

## Soil Sampling Methods

All these projects involve collecting a number of soil samples. Take a sample from an exposed section or simply cut away the vegetation and take a sample of the topsoil with a garden trowel. Except for depth surveys, which are done using a soil auger as shown in Photo 6, it is best to do any tests on soil samples back in school.

Photo 6. Using a soil auger

Soil is best collected as follows:

1. Scoop up a level trowelful and put it inside a tough polythene bag. Freezer bags are ideal as you can write the number and location of your sample on the outside.
2. Seal the bag very tightly to prevent moisture loss.
3. For each sample fill in a booking-sheet like the one shown in Fig. 17.

Fig. 17. Booking sheet for soil samples

| Site number | Grid reference | Height (from map) | Slope angle and shape | Aspect | Geology (from map) | Vegetation type | Land use | Weather during last 24 h | Depth measured with auger | Comments on drainage |
|---|---|---|---|---|---|---|---|---|---|---|
| 1 | 638721 | 207 m | 0°, flat | Level hilltop | Millstone grit | Peat | Moorland | Heavy rain | Over 100cm, didn't reach bedrock | Poorly drained, peat hags |
| 2 | 638756 | 186 m | 14°, concave | SW | Shale | Heather, bilberries | Moorland | Heavy rain, soil very wet | 19 cm | Shedding site on hillside |

# INVESTIGATING SOILS

## Guide to Testing Soil Characteristics

Table 5. How to analyse soil characteristics

| Soil characteristic | Significance | Means of analysis |
|---|---|---|
| pH | Measure of soil acidity, which is the most important chemical characteristic of soil and affects both vegetation and land use and most soil-forming processes | B.D.H. kit<br>Probe |
| Texture | Measure of size of particles which make up the soil, therefore affects drainage and amount of air present in soil | Mechanical analysis<br>Sieves<br>Texture chart |
| Chemicals | Elements such as potassium, sodium and nitrogen provide food for plants | Sudbury kit – a cheap 'Test Your Garden' type is available |
| Colour | Results from the minerals which form the soil – a red colour comes from oxidized (rusty) iron | Home-made chart |
| Water content (moisture) | Soil water provides plants with essential water and transports nutrients | Laboratory experiments  Probe |
| Humus content | Humus helps the soil remain fertile | Laboratory experiment |
| Temperature | Important for the growth and germination of plants | In the **field** using a thermometer |
| Bulk density | Shows the amount of compaction of the soil and the effect of ploughing and trampling | Laboratory experiment |

Table 5 shows you the major characteristics of soil which you can test and explains their significance. You can also see how the analysis can be done.

## Soil pH

The pH is a measure of the concentration of hydrogen ions – the greater the concentration, the more acid the soil. The pH is measured on a scale from 1 to 14 with the low numbers indicating an acid soil, a pH of 7 being neutral and numbers above 7 indicating alkalinity. Soil acidity greatly affects the plant life as shown in Fig. 18. Farmers often add lime to their fields to make the soil less acid.

Fig. 19 shows how to test the pH of the soil using a standard soil-testing kit.

Fig. 18. Significance of soil acidity to plants

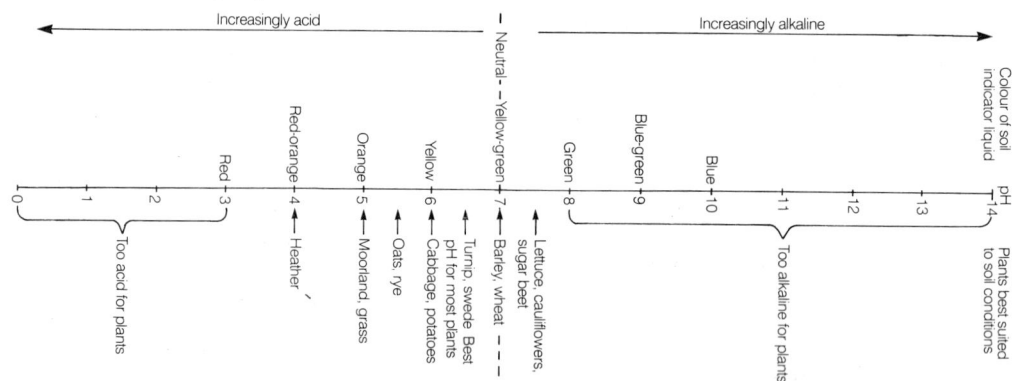

# INVESTIGATING SOILS

Fig. 19. How to measure the pH of a soil

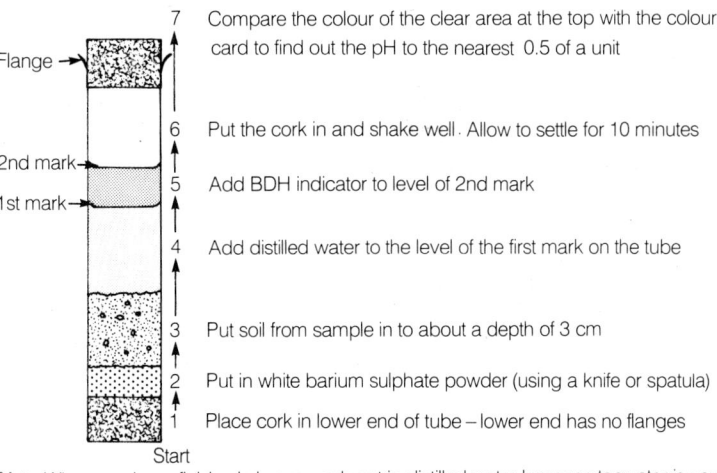

**Note** When you have finished always wash out in distilled water because tapwater is usually slightly acid.

## Soil Texture

Soil particles are classified into three main groups according to their diameter:

1. **Sand**   diameter 0.2 mm – 2 mm.
2. **Silt**   diameter 0.002 mm – 0.2 mm.
3. **Clay**   diameter less than 0.002 mm.

A soil with roughly equal proportions of sand, silt and clay is called a **loam**. It is possible to gauge the texture of a soil by handling a soil sample:

**Sand** feels gritty, and if there is a high percentage, you can hear the sand grains grating against each other.
**Silt** feels silky and smooth, and when there is a lot of silt, the soil feels rather like the inside of a quilt.
**Clay** is sticky and makes the soil particles cling together. The following easy tests give you some idea of the percentage of clay present when working with a dry soil:
25% clay – soil forms rings with no breaks.
20% clay – soil leaves a smooth polished skin on fingers.
10 – 15% clay – soil can be rolled into rods or sausages.
5% clay – soil sample can be made into a cube.

Another way is to rely on Stokes' Law, which states that the larger the diameter of a particle the quicker it will settle. First put 200 g of dry soil into a dry jam jar and measure the height the soil sample reaches up the side. Then fill the jar with water and shake vigorously. Measure the depth of particles on the bottom after 50 s to find the percentage of sand, after 8 h to find the percentage of silt, and after three days to find the percentage of clay.

When you have completed your texture tests you can use the triangular graph in Fig. 20 to find the soil group of your sample.

Fig. 20. Triangular graph to show soil texture

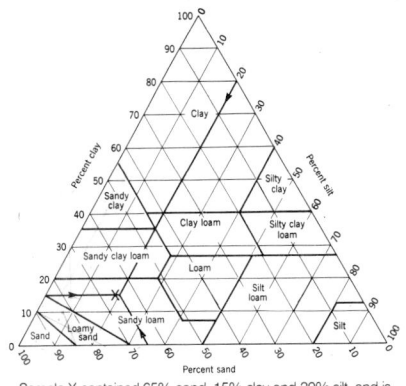

Sample X contained 65% sand, 15% clay and 20% silt, and is therefore a sandy loam.

# INVESTIGATING SOILS

## Soil Chemicals

The levels of nitrogen, phosphorus and potash can be tested using standard kits such as the Sudbury Kit. These are sold in garden centres. Special solutions are put on top of soil contained in a test tube and the results matched with a colour chart. The tests show which elements are lacking in the soil; when you are doing land-use surveys it is very useful to relate this to the farmer's fertilizer policy and the crop yields per hectare.

## Soil Colour

This can be measured by matching the soil sample with a home-made chart. Obtain a range of paint colour charts covering the nine colours listed in Fig. 21. Colour charts for stonework paint are ideal. To gain a good comparison place the soil on the colour chart itself and find the best match.

## Soil Water Content

Water content can be measured really accurately only in the laboratory. You can buy a cheap soil moisture probe which is very suitable for surveying a wide area efficiently and enables you to make a map of soil moisture variations which can be related to slope and geology.*

The laboratory method of measuring soil water content is:

1. Weigh an empty heat-proof dish (e.g. 100 g).
2. Put a small sample (about 50 g) of soil into the dish and weigh soil and dish together (e.g. 150 g).
3. Put the dish of soil into an oven at 110°C (230°F or gas mark 3) overnight.
4. Weigh the dish of now dry soil (e.g. 145 g).

This is how you calculate the moisture content of the soil using the results given above:

Weight of water in soil = 150 g – 145 g = 5 g.
Weight of wet soil = 150 g – 100 g = 50 g.
Percentage moisture content = $\frac{5}{50} \times 100 = 10\%$.

*See *Teaching Geography*, vol. 9 (1984), p.4 for method.

Fig. 21. Home-made soil colour chart

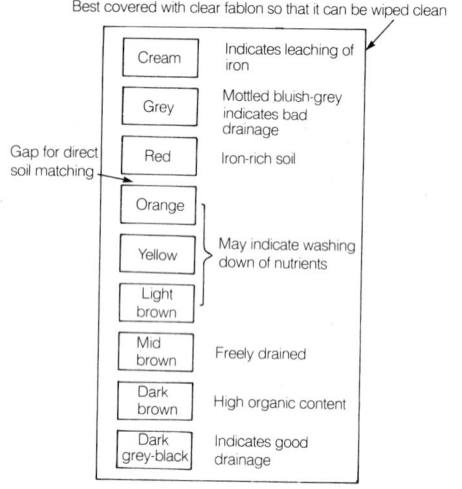

## Soil Humus Content

This must be found using dry soil so it is best to do this experiment straight after you have measured the moisture content. The method is as follows:

1. Grind up the soil and weigh it in the same heat-proof dish to check the weight of the dry soil.
2. Heat the dish containing the soil sample over a bunsen burner for half an hour to burn off the organic matter.
3. Weigh the dish and burned soil and calculate the weight of soil after burning.
4. Find the weight loss after burning. This gives you the weight of the lost organic matter.

The formula below will give you the humus content, which is usually somewhere between 1% and 12% although peat soil may be up to 80% organic matter:

humus content (%) = $\frac{\text{weight loss after burning}}{\text{weight of dry unburned soil}} \times 100$.

## Safety

- Always work in a laboratory supervised by a teacher.

# INVESTIGATING SOILS

## Soil Compaction

Studying the effect of a footpath, heavy farm machinery, or cattle upon the soil will require you to see how compacted the soil has become. You would expect the air to have been forced out of the soil by the weight of the cattle, etc. Measuring how compacted the soil has become is straightforward. The idea is to compare the weight of identical volumes of soil. Heavier samples have had more air squeezed out of them and are therefore more compacted.

Photo 7. Taking a core sample

Hammer a tube about 15 cm long and 4 cm in diameter into the soil to obtain the sample as shown in Photo 7. Dry the soil as described on page 22 then weigh it. The compaction, called the **bulk density**, is given by the formula bulk density (g/c.c.) = 

$$\frac{\text{weight of dry soil (g)}}{\text{volume of soil in tube (c.c.)}}$$

The larger the result, the greater the degree of compaction. Compaction measurements taken across a footpath are a useful part of a project investigating the effects of human activity in an area.

## Soil-profile Studies

In order to understand what a soil is like we need to look below the surface. This can be done either by finding a place where the soil is exposed (e.g. a river bank or quarry) or by digging a pit. Obtain permission from the landowner before digging and be sure to replace all the soil and vegetation.

Photo 8. Soil horizons

Photo 8 shows how the soil is made up of layers, called **horizons**. Horizons can be identified by their different colours and textures.

Fig. 22. How to label a soil profile

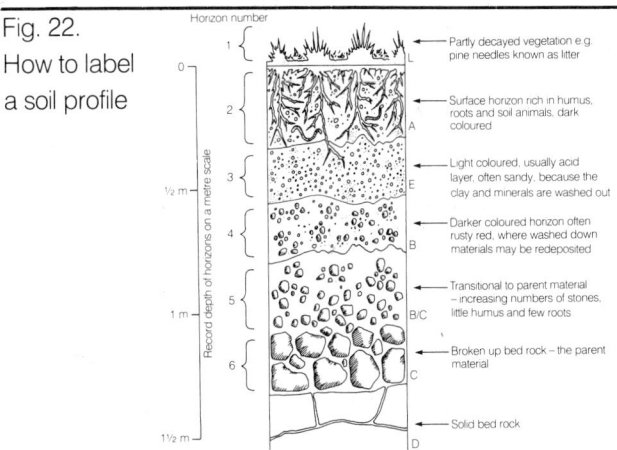

Fig. 22 indicates some of the changes you would expect to find within a soil profile and shows you how to recognize the main horizons. Your soil profile may have as few as two main horizons, but most soils have three or four. First try to distinguish the actual horizons in your profile, then measure the depth of each and record its characteristics.

# INVESTIGATING SOILS

Fig. 23. Booking sheet for soil profile characteristics

| Horizon number | Possible letter | Average depth (cm) | Nature of boundary | Colour | Texture by feel | Stoniness (%) | Roots (%) | Fauna | Sample taken ✓ or ✗ | pH | Laboratory tests |   |
|---|---|---|---|---|---|---|---|---|---|---|---|---|
|   |   |   |   |   |   |   |   |   |   |   | Moisture content | Humus content |
| 1 | L | 2 | Clear | Dark brown | Silty | None | High, full of leaves | None | ✓ |   |   |   |
| 2 | A | 15 | Merging | Dark brown | Silty clay | 1 | High | 2 worms | ✓ |   |   |   |

## How to Analyse the Results of a Soil Transect

The two main aims are:
1. To identify the changes which occur along the transect.
2. To identify any relationships which may help explain the changes.

If you draw graphs of your results as in Fig. 24, any changes will be clear. For example, Graph A shows that soil acidity increases the higher up the slope you go.

Graph B tests the strength of the link between slope angle and soil acidity. A positive correlation is indicated; that is, as slopes become steeper, the soil becomes more acidic. Graph C shows a negative correlation indicating that as slopes become steeper, soil depth becomes shallower. To be really accurate you could use a mathematical correlation technique (see Book 1) to test the strength of the relationship.

Take a trowelful of soil from each horizon and seal it in a labelled polythene bag for laboratory tests. At each site also make a note of the vegetation and drainage.

The best way of presenting your results is either by drawing a scale soil-profile diagram as in Fig. 22 or, even better, by making a mini-profile in the following way:

1. Draw out the profile to scale, e.g. with 1 cm on the paper representing 10 cm of soil depth, and mark on the horizons.
2. Smear soil from each horizon in the space drawn out to get the correct impression of the colour, or cover your drawing of the profile with thick strong glue then deposit loose soil from the sample of each horizon you have collected. Seal with sellotape to stop bits falling off.
3. Label each horizon fully.

Fig. 24. The results of a soil transect

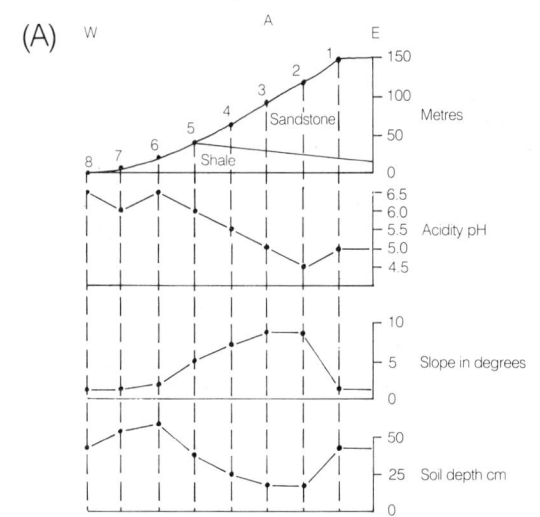

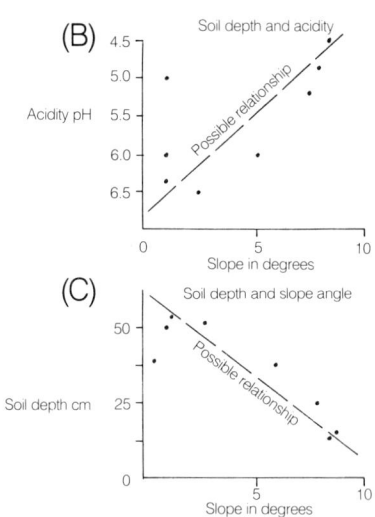

# INVESTIGATING THE VEGETATION

Vegetation studies provide excellent projects. You do not have to know a lot about biology, but you do have to be prepared to use a **flora** – a pictorial guide which helps you to identify any grasses or plant types present. Simple guides such as the *Observer's Books* are ideal. Grasses are particularly difficult to recognize.

There are very few areas in Britain where the vegetation can be said to be 'natural'; even the moors have been greatly affected by grazing and by burning by gamekeepers. It is obviously best to do your vegetation surveys in the countryside, avoiding artificial parks and gardens.

## Project Ideas

1. Vegetation surveys can be made across an area of varied countryside. This is known as a **vegetation transect**, from which you aim to make a detailed record of the nature of the vegetation.
2. Woodland surveys can investigate either variations in vegetation and microclimate, or the structure of the woodland or the impact of human activity.
3. Hedgerow surveys can investigate the age of hedges and the variations in their nature and frequency caused by both environmental and human factors.

Fig. 25. How to recognize the main layers of vegetation

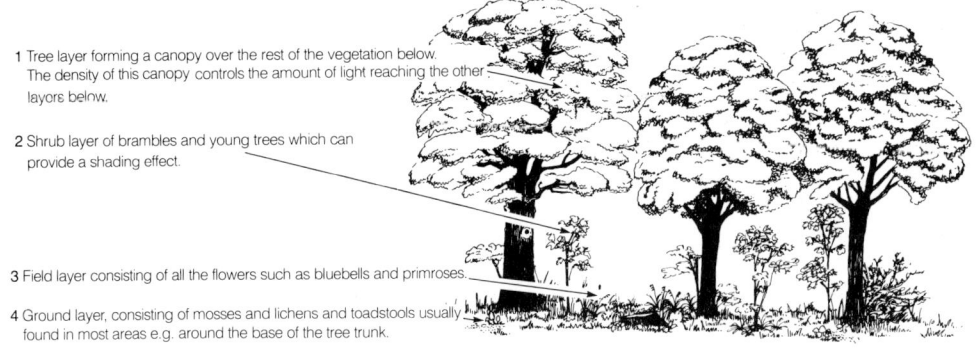

1 Tree layer forming a canopy over the rest of the vegetation below. The density of this canopy controls the amount of light reaching the other layers below.
2 Shrub layer of brambles and young trees which can provide a shading effect.
3 Field layer consisting of all the flowers such as bluebells and primroses.
4 Ground layer, consisting of mosses and lichens and toadstools usually found in most areas e.g. around the base of the tree trunk.

Vegetation, especially in woods, consists of a number of layers, called **strata**. Fig. 25 shows you what to look for. In most cases, you will be studying only the field layer, with grasses, herbs and flowering plants. One of the main problems is to work out a way of actually sampling the vegetation, as areas may contain hundreds of individual plants. You need a reliable estimate of the vegetation without surveying the whole area. The problem can be tackled in two ways, either by using quadrats or by using transect lines.

## Equipment Check-list

The exact items will vary for each project. However the main ones are :

- Quadrat.
- Polythene bags for soil samples.
- Reference book to help you identify the plants.
- Booking-sheets.
- Wide sellotape for securing small samples of vegetation.

# INVESTIGATING THE VEGETATION

## Before You Begin

Vegetation studies are done either by transects, which means following a route across an area, or by point samples at a number of separate sites. Both involve crossing privately owned land. Always obtain the land-owner's permission *before* you start.

Your survey line or points should cover a number of contrasting areas (different rock type, height, slope, etc.) and avoid too much cultivated land. Have a good look around before you finally decide which is the best location for the study. Beforehand collect samples of the common types of vegetation and make yourself a Fablon-covered key with the names of these plants clearly labelled. There will probably be about fifteen common species.

## How to Sample Vegetation
### Point Samples

Decide on the number of points needed to provide an accurate survey. One rough rule to follow is that if you keep finding new plant types (known as species) in apparently similar areas near to each other then your sample is too small. As a general rule survey as many points as time permits.

The placing of these survey points is also very important as it affects the nature of your sample. Fig. 26 explains how to ensure that you select the correct places to do your survey. You must take samples from each different area of vegetation. One random method that works well is to walk through the area for five minutes, changing direction every minute. Where you end up is your sampling point.

Fig. 26. Methods of sampling woodland vegetation

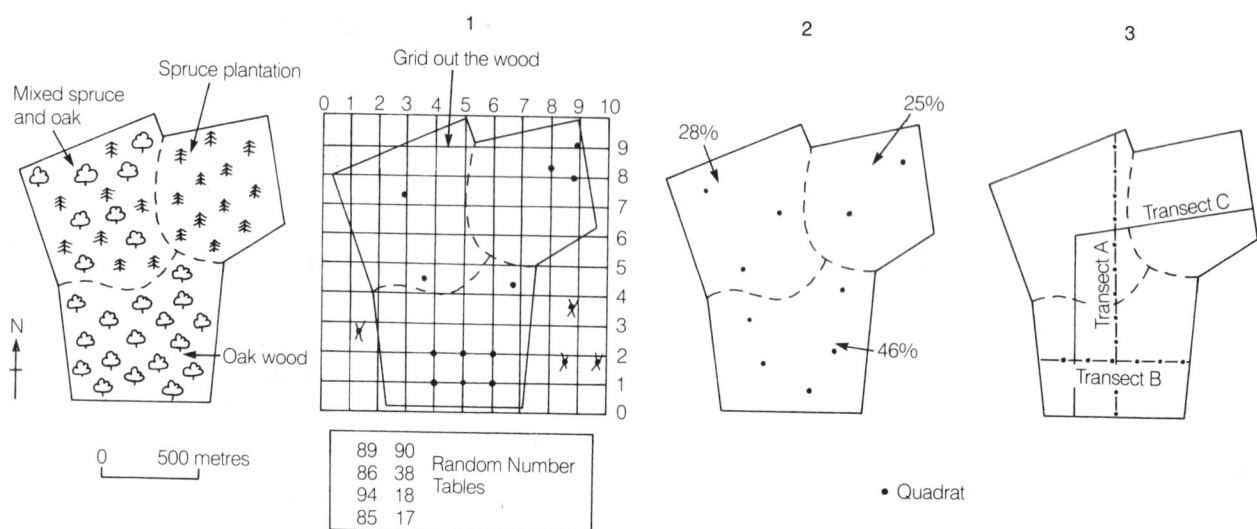

The sketch shows a typical small wooded area and the various ways you could sample the vegetation.

1 Shows random sampling – from random number tables. The problem is that in the first 10 samples only 6 occur in the wood, and none in the southern area. The position would improve if you take 25 samples.

2 In this case there is an attempt to cover the wood with the number of samples in each of the three areas being related to the size of each woodland area. 5/10 samples in the oak wood which covers ½ the area. These could be random.

3 Shows the problems of siting transects. You must carry out an initial survey as only transect C covers all three sections of the wood.

# INVESTIGATING THE VEGETATION

## By Transects

Fig. 26 explains how to decide on the best location for a transect. Transect lines are usually at right angles to each other but in areas like sand dunes it is best to survey just one straight-line transect.

You also have to decide how often to stop and record the vegetation along the transect. Where plants are widely spaced as in a wood, stop every 10 m; in grassland 1 m is the correct spacing. The best method is a belt transect as in Fig. 27. You sketch the vegetation present in a belt, say 2 m wide, along the length of the transect.

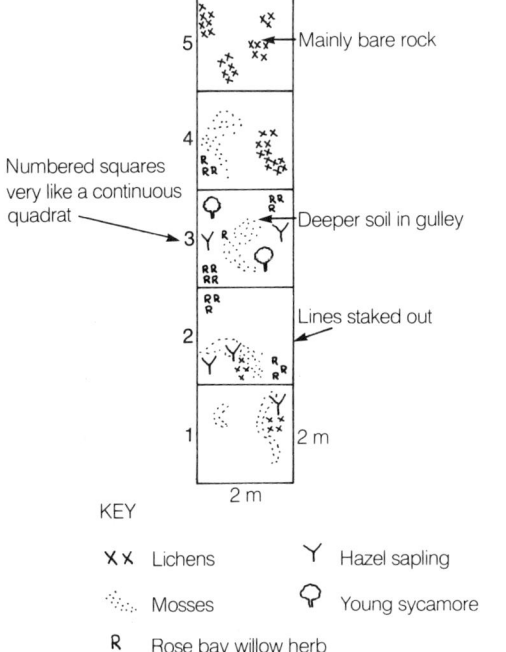

Fig. 27. A belt transect across a quarry

KEY
x x  Lichens            Y  Hazel sapling
     Mosses             ♀  Young sycamore
R    Rose bay willow herb

## What to Record at Each Site

Whatever method you choose in order to decide where your survey sites should be, the information to be collected is the same. Use a quadrat at each site to help you make the observations listed on the booking-sheet (Fig. 29).

A quadrat is a frame enclosing an area of known size – usually a square. For surveying grassland and moorland ½ m × ½ m is a useful size although in woodland 20 m × 20 m is required. You can make a quadrat out of wood or coloured chicken-wire as shown in Fig. 28. The quadrat can be subdivided using string, to provide further sampling sites.

Fig. 28. Making a quadrat

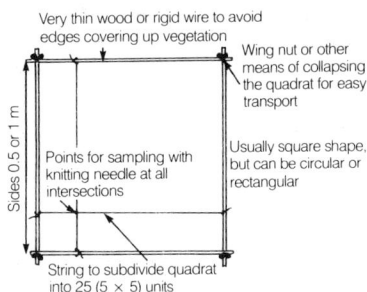

## Number of Occurrences of Each Plant Species

Poke a knitting-needle into the ground and record the plant(s) you find at that point. Investigate either 25 random samples (just shut your eyes and poke the ground) or 25 selected samples.

## Percentage Cover of Each Plant Species

Estimate the percentage cover of each species by eye. Make sure you take into account the roots as well as the leaves. You can then use the table in Fig. 29 to convert the percentage to a cover value. Always record the percentage cover of bare ground.

## Frequency of Each Plant Species

The frequency of a plant type is a measure of how common it is. For instance, if you had twenty quadrats in a moorland area of your transect and ten contained a particular plant type, the frequency would equal
$$\frac{10}{20} \times 100 = 50\%.$$

# INVESTIGATING THE VEGETATION

Fig. 29. Booking sheet for vegetation transect

| Station number | 3 | Grid Ref. | 627358 | Height | 283 m above sea-level |
| --- | --- | --- | --- | --- | --- |
| Aspect | SW | Slope Angle | 17° | Slope Shape/Drainage | Concave, wet receiving site |
| Geology | Gritstone | Soil Sample | ✓ | Soil Depth | 53 cm |
| Wind Speed | N/A | Temperature | N/A | Land Use | Rough pasture/fell |

Observations on site __Very marshy__

### Vegetation Species

| Name | Number Present (occurrences) | Estimated % Cover | Cover Value |
| --- | --- | --- | --- |
| 1. Heather | ⊬⊬ II | 40% | 3 |
| 2. Cotton grass | III | 10% | 1 |
| 3. Rushes | I | 0% | 0 |
| 4. | | | |
| 5. | | | |
| 6. | | | |
| 7. | | | |
| 8. | | | |
| 9. Bare ground | ⊬⊬ ⊬⊬ IIII | 50% | 4 |

Space for sellotaping sample of any unknown species

Sketch of Quadrat 3

| Reference chart for Cover Values | Cover Value |
| --- | --- |
| Present but cover negligible | 0 |
| Cover of 0 to 10% | 1 |
| Cover of 10 to 25% | 2 |
| Cover of 25 to 50% | 3 |
| Cover of 50 to 75% | 4 |
| Cover of over 75% | 5 |

How to estimate percentage cover
- Each square worth 1%
- Sketch of vegetation pattern
- Total of about 40% heather
- 50% bare ground
- 9% cotton grass

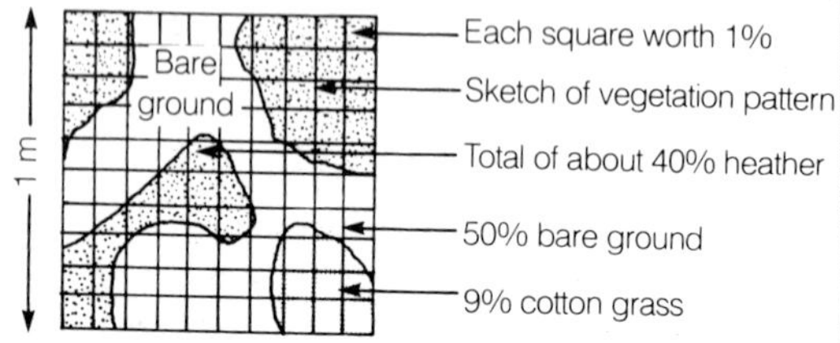

## Presenting the Results of a Vegetation Survey
### Vegetation Variations

First put all the results for your transect on a booking-sheet similar to Fig. 29. Then use bar charts to illustrate the variations in number of occurrences or percentage cover of species along the transect.

Fig. 30 shows an example of a **kite diagram**; the process of construction can be seen if you look at Stations 29 – 33 for bluebells. At Station 30, bluebells formed 46% of the cover so an area representing 23% – is shaded each side of the horizontal axis. This type of graph shows relationships over the transect very clearly and can be used also to show variations in frequency and number of occurrences.

# INVESTIGATING THE VEGETATION

Fig. 30. Kite diagram showing variations in vegetation cover

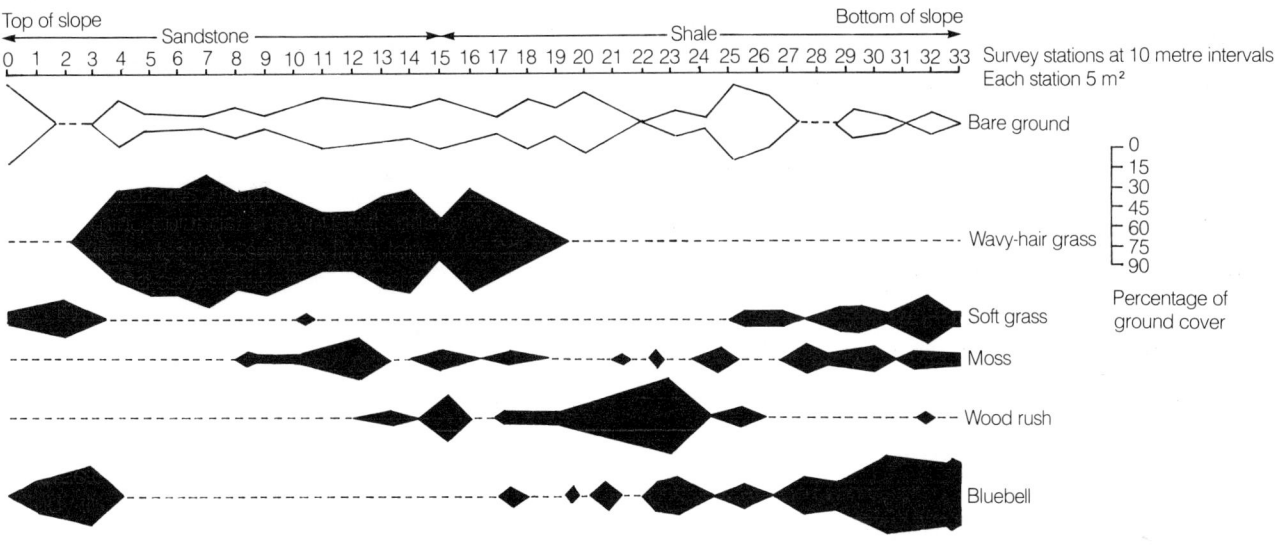

The variation in species for individual sample points can be clearly shown by star diagrams as in Fig. 31. You have to decide on the main species present, preferably the eight most important.

## *Vegetation Associations*

Many plants often grow very close to only a few other species. For example, sphagnum moss and reeds usually grow side by side. This is a **vegetation association**.

A simple method of identifying associations is to write the names of all the plant species in your survey in a big circle, as if around the rim of a wheel. Go through your results and every time two plants are found in the same quadrat join their names with a line of 1 mm thickness. Those plants in close association will stand out by being joined together by thick lines. Fig. 32 shows that buttercups and clover have a close association.

Your teacher may have more advanced books which explain how to describe vegetation association statistically, as well as access to computer software which will help you to handle the data.

Fig. 31. Star diagram showing ground cover plants

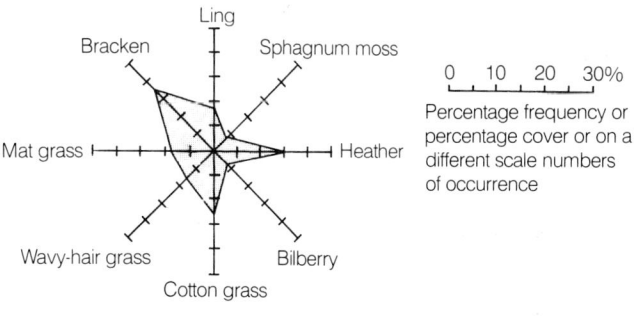

Fig. 32. An association diagram

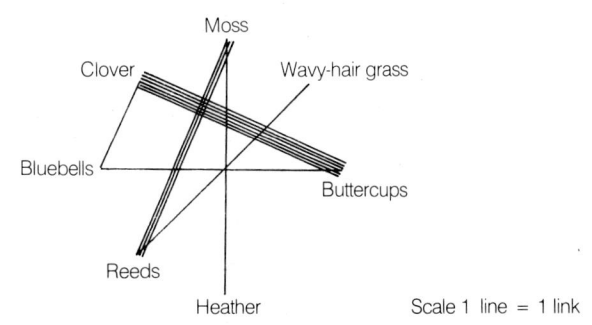

# INVESTIGATING THE VEGETATION

## Relating the Vegetation Distribution to Environmental Factors

It is useful to summarize the environmental changes on a diagram in a similar way to that shown for a soil transect in Fig. 24. You can then take individual plant types, especially those occurring commonly, and relate their distribution to particular environmental factors. You will need to complete soil tests as shown on pages 20 – 22 to do this. Fig. 33, which is a scattergram, shows that heather is restricted to very acid soils in contrast to bracken and fescue grass. This method of analysis can be repeated for other factors such as slope angle, soil moisture, etc.

## Woodland Survey

Make a detailed survey of two contrasting woods not more than 1 km² in size, or one larger varied wood not more than 3 km² in size. For both projects you will need to carry out detailed sampling of the wood either by use of large staked-out quadrats, or by use of the belt transect techniques described on page 27.

Fig. 33. Scattergram showing plant type and soil acidity

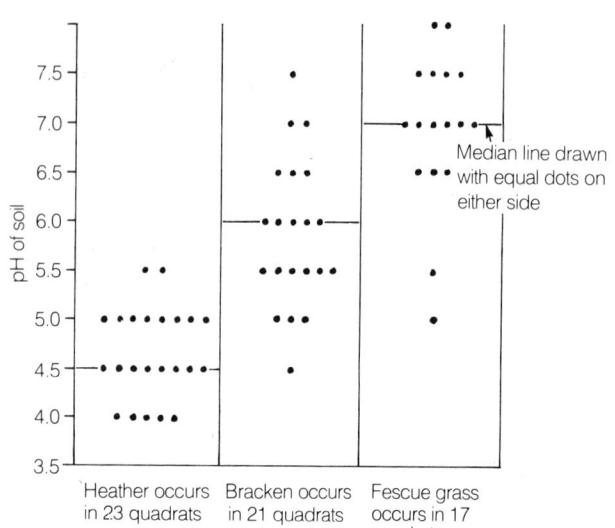

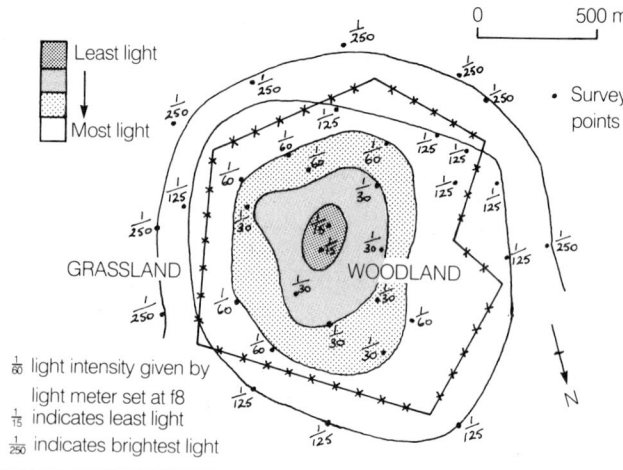

Fig. 34. Isopleth map showing variations in light intensity

## Project Ideas

You can collect detailed information to show the following aspects:
1. The variations in the environment and microclimate within the woodland, to include temperature distribution, drainage, soil pH, depth, moisture and humus content, light intensity, etc.
2. The structure of the woodland, to include tree-type variations, age, size, density, and the layering of the vegetation within the wood.
3. The effect of man's activities, such as trampling, within the woodland.

When you decide on your project you need to select the information you require to cover one of the above topics. You will find details of many of the techniques available elsewhere in the book.

## Contrasts in Woodland

Tree type obviously affects the light intensity, rainfall, wind strength, humidity, temperature and soil type. Using the methods described elsewhere in this book you can easily survey these aspects of a wood. The results can be displayed using maps like Fig. 34, which shows variations in light intensity measured using a light meter.

# INVESTIGATING THE VEGETATION

## The Nature and Structure of Woodland

Tree type can be surveyed by making a large general map of the woodland and recording the general distribution of the main tree types. You can then sample selected quadrats to work out the density of trees per unit area. You should also record the number of occurrences of trees of various types – the results can be presented by pie chart. The **dominant** type is the one which occurs as a mature tree most commonly and may vary within the wood: sometimes two or three types of tree are equally important and are said to be **co-dominants**. It is possible to use nearest-neighbour techniques (see Book 6) to describe statistically the pattern of the major trees.

Photo 9. Measuring the girth of a tree

The **age** of a wood can sometimes be found by looking at old maps of the area, which may show when the woodland was planted. It is also possible to measure the circumference of a tree, termed the **girth**, as shown in Photo 9 and to calculate the age of that particular tree. Table 6 lists the average increase in girth made each year by ten common trees. In Photo 9 the tree is an oak with a girth of 64 cm. The age of the oak is therefore

$\frac{64}{1.88}$ = 34 years.

In order to obtain reliable results you should repeat this measurement for several mature trees within your quadrat, as it is very likely they will have been planted at a similar time.

Table 6. Increase in girth per year of common British trees within a mixed woodland

| Oak | 1.88 cm |
| Hazel, ash, elm, beech | 2.5 cm |
| Sycamore | 2.75 cm |
| Holly, yew | 1.25 cm |
| Pine, spruce (average) | 3.13 cm |

## Human Activity

Assessing human damage to woodland involves using techniques which also apply to other types of vegetation crossed by a series of well-used footpaths. Fig. 35 shows the various features to look out for when considering the stability of a vegetated area. The techniques are similar to those for other vegetation surveys; carry out transects *across* footpaths. Continue each transect for 10 m on each side of the path, recording all the damaging effects visible. These types of observation can form part of a much wider pollution or tourism survey.

Fig. 35. How to recognize whether vegetation is growing, declining or stable

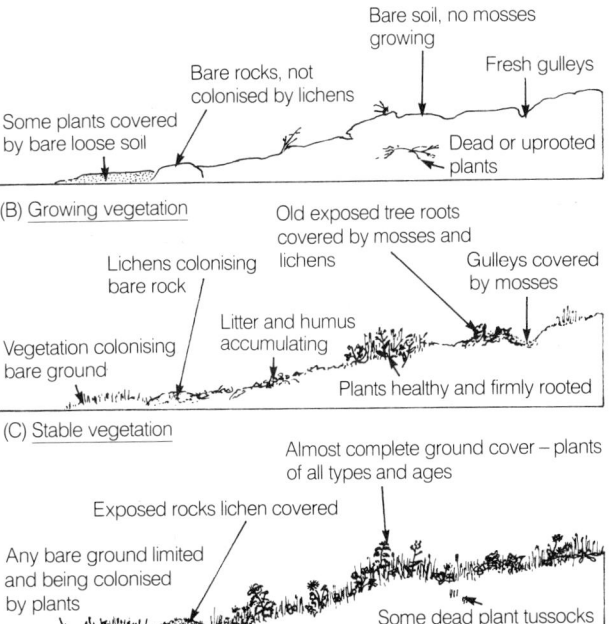

31

# INVESTIGATING THE VEGETATION

## How to Carry out a Hedgerow Survey

A hedgerow survey is a specialized transect, usually done over a distance of 30 m, where you record the number of shrubs, herbs and ground-layer species. Information can be presented either as a transect diagram similar to Fig. 27 or as a composite section like Fig. 36 describing the species occurring in the 30 m stretch of hedgerow. Fig. 36 has the advantage of showing the effects of aspect. Note how the sunny south-facing side has a much greater variety of herbs than the darker, moister north-facing side. You could also add details of the number of occurrences of each species.

If the hedgerow has been unaffected by spraying, cutting, etc., it is possible to tell its age. On average, every 100 years one new species of shrub (*not* plant type) colonizes a hedgerow. Therefore a hedgerow containing eight different shrubs within 30 m is 800 years old. An interesting survey is to look at old maps and record ancient field boundaries. As a result of the need for large fields owing to mechanization, many farmers have destroyed hedgerows. By going round the fields, mapping today's hedges and comparing them with those shown on old maps, you can clearly see the amount of change.

Another idea is to compare the nature of hedgerows in two different areas, perhaps one of arable farming and one of livestock farming. This project will involve asking the farmers about their policy towards hedgerows, so do check that they are willing to talk to you before you begin.

Fig. 36. Species survey of a hedgerow

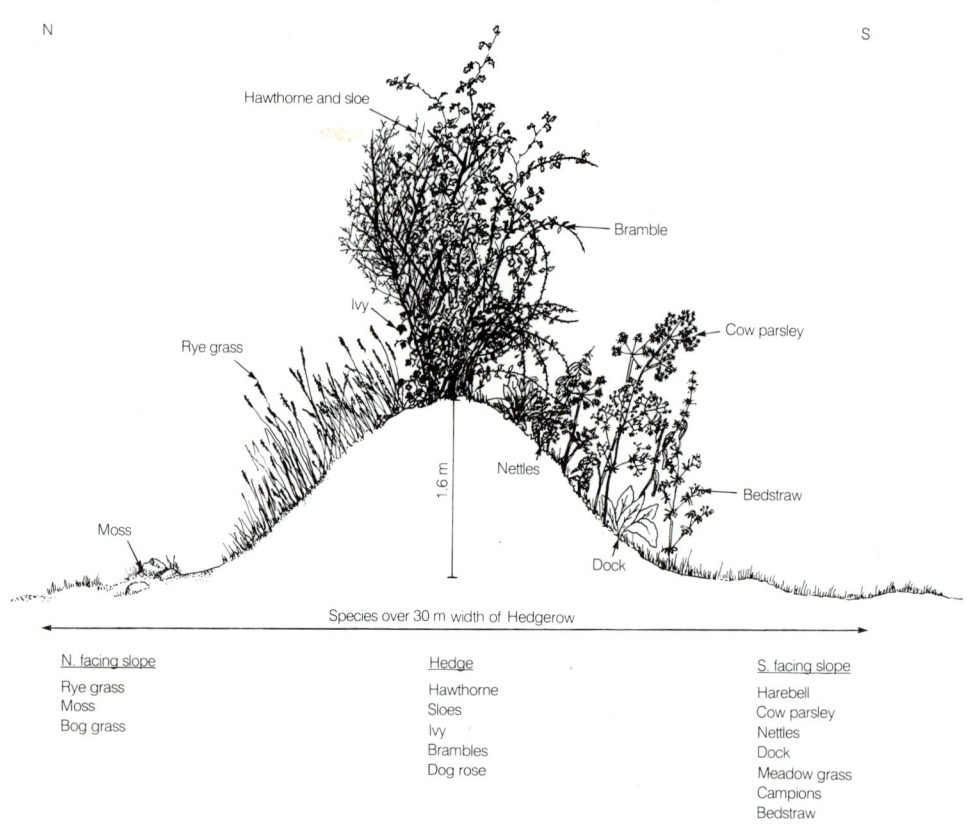

| N. facing slope | Hedge | S. facing slope |
|---|---|---|
| Rye grass | Hawthorne | Harebell |
| Moss | Sloes | Cow parsley |
| Bog grass | Ivy | Nettles |
| | Brambles | Dock |
| | Dog rose | Meadow grass |
| | | Campions |
| | | Bedstraw |